Investigations and Projects Masters

Mathematics
Applications and Connections

Course 2

 **Glencoe McGraw-Hill**

New York, New York   Columbus, Ohio   Woodland Hills, California   Peoria, Illinois

Glencoe/McGraw-Hill

A Division of The **McGraw·Hill** Companies

Send all inquiries to:
Glencoe/McGraw-Hill
936 Eastwind Drive
Westerville, Ohio 43081-3329

ISBN: 0-02-833088-9   *Investigations and Projects Masters,* Course 2

  3 4 5 6 7 8 9 10   045   05 04 03 02 01 00 99

Contents

Interdisciplinary Investigation

(Student Edition, Pages 128–129)

If the Shoe Fits...

MATERIALS

- Recording Sheet master, p. 4
- tape measure
- calculator

OVERVIEW

In this investigation, students will collect and analyze data, and design a method to display the results. You may want to suggest that students use grid paper or other tools to help them construct their graphs. Make a copy of the Recording Sheet master on page 4 for each student.

PROCEDURE

1. Encourage students to measure both boys and girls throughout the age range given. Here are some possible discussion questions.
   - Should you measure in millimeters, centimeters, or meters?
   - Should the length be from the big toe to the heel?
   - What if there is another toe that is longer than the big toe?
   - Should you measure with shoes on, with socks on, or without socks?
2. Briefly review how to find the mean, median, mode, and range.
3. Briefly review the various type of graphs that students have studied.
4. You may want to give students parameters for writing their concluding statement. Some things to specify are length of statement, key words to include, format, and so on.

OUTSIDE RESOURCES

Edelson, Edward. *Genetics and Heredity*. New York: Chelsea House, 1990.

Gay, Kathlyn. *Caution! This May Be an Advertisement: A Teen Guide to Advertising*. New York: Franklin Watts, 1992.

Mitchell, Barbara. *Shoes for Everyone: A Story About Jan Matzeliger*. Minneapolis: Carolrhoda Books, 1986.

Silverstein, Alvin and Virginia B. Silverstein. *The Story of Your Foot*. New York: Putnam, 1987.

Interdisciplinary Investigation

(Student Edition, Pages 128–129)

If the Shoe Fits...

PROCEDURE

Person	Length (Boys)	Length (Girls)	Length (Boys & Girls)
1		18 cm	
2	23 cm		
3	20 cm		
4		17 cm	
5		20 cm	
6	25 cm		
7	23 cm		
8		16 cm	
9		16 cm	
10	19 cm		
Mean	22 cm	17.4 cm	19.7 cm
Median	23 cm	17 cm	19.5 cm
Mode	23 cm	16 cm	16, 20, and 23 cm
Range	6 cm	4 cm	9 cm

MAKING THE CONNECTION

Language Arts Predictions should reflect the distribution of sizes from the data. Advertisements should appeal to the targeted consumer group.

Social Studies The paper should explain who Jan Earnst Matzeliger was and what he did for the shoe industry. Statistics should be accurate and organized.

Science The description should explain how a Punnett Square is used. An example should be included using the data to make a prediction.

GO FURTHER

- Data should be well organized and reflect a wide distribution of age groups. The graphs should be well labeled and accurately represent the data.
- The podiatrist's name and the information from the medical charts should be included along with a statement comparing the findings to the charts.

2

Interdisciplinary Investigation

(Student Edition, Pages 128–129)

If the Shoe Fits...

Level	Specific Criteria
3 Superior	● Shows a thorough understanding of the concepts of *mean, median, mode,* and *range.*
	● Uses appropriate strategies to solve problems.
	● Computations are correct.
	● Written explanations are exemplary.
	● Charts, model, and any statements included are appropriate and sensible.
	● Goes beyond the requirements of some or all problems.
2 Satisfactory, with minor flaws	● Shows understanding of the concepts of *mean, median, mode,* and *range.*
	● Uses appropriate strategies to solve problems.
	● Computations are mostly correct.
	● Written explanations are effective.
	● Charts, model, and any statements included are appropriate and sensible.
	● Satisfies the requirements of problems.
1 Nearly Satisfactory, with obvious flaws	● Shows understanding of most of the concepts of *mean, median, mode,* and *range.*
	● May not use appropriate strategies to solve problems.
	● Computations are mostly correct.
	● Written explanations are satisfactory.
	● Charts, model, and any statements included are appropriate and sensible.
	● Satisfies the requirements of problems.
0 Unsatisfactory	● Shows little or no understanding of the concepts of *mean, median, mode,* and *range.*
	● Does not use appropriate strategies to solve problems.
	● Computations are incorrect.
	● Written explanations are not satisfactory.
	● Charts, model, and any statements included are not appropriate or sensible.
	● Does not satisfy the requirements of the problems.

Interdisciplinary Investigation

(Student Edition, Pages 128–129)

If the Shoe Fits...

Use this table to record your data.

Person	Length (Boys)	Length (Girls)	Length (Boys & Girls)
Mean			
Median			
Mode			
Range			

Display your results in a graph.

Write a concluding statement that describes the data.

Interdisciplinary Investigation

(Student Edition, Pages 264–265)

"A" is for Apple

MATERIALS

- Recording Sheet master, p. 8
- magazine
- calculator
- photocopy machine
- highlighters

OVERVIEW

In this investigation, students will collect data from printed materials that they use every day. They will determine which letters are most common and then design their own letter set. Make a copy of the Recording Sheet master on page 8 for each student.

PROCEDURE

1. Have students work in groups of three or four. Have each member select a page of written text from a newspaper, magazine, or book. Photocopy the selected page and use a marker to highlight 80 to 100 consecutive words to be used in the investigation.

2. Each member of the group should tally the number of times each letter appears in their text sample along with the total number of letters in the sample.

3. You may want to review converting ratios to percents.

4. You may want to have students design their letter sets for a specific type of business.

OUTSIDE RESOURCES

Burnley, David. *A History of the English Language.* New York, NY: Longman Publisher, 1992.

Byron, Theodora. *Historical Linguistics.* New York, NY: Cambridge University Press, 1993.

Crystal, David. *The Cambridge Encyclopedia of the English Language.* New York, NY: Cambridge University Press, 1995.

Interdisciplinary Investigation

(Student Edition, Pages 264–265)

"A" is for Apple

PROCEDURE

1. Text sample: Hurricanes are violent storms that form over water in the zone of the Trade Winds. They produce strong winds, high seas, …

2.

Letter	Number of Times in Text	Ratio Out of 459 Letters	Ratio as %
A	41	41:459	8.9
B	6	6:459	1.3
⋮	⋮	⋮	⋮
Y	7	7:459	1.5
Z	1	1:459	0.2

3. Sample answer: In the sample text, the letter E is the most common. The letters Q and J are the least common.

4. The letter set should contain the number of letters that correspond with the percent found in the group data table. Sample answer:
9-A, 1-B, 5-C, 4-D, 11-E, 2-F, 1-G, 6-H, 9-I, 1-J, 1-K, 3-L, 3-M, 8-N, 7-O, 2-P, 1-Q, 8-R, 6-S, 9-T, 2-U, 1-V, 2-W, 1-X, 2-Y, 1-Z

MAKING THE CONNECTION

Language Arts   You may wish to use a textbook of the foreign language or consult with a teacher in the foreign language department to be sure that any non-English letters are included in the table.

Music   Group students who cannot read music with students who can to complete this section. Percents should represent the ratio of each note to the notes on the entire page.

Social Studies   The report on alphabetic writing and Phoenician writing should be accurate and cite the information source.

GO FURTHER

- Answers should reflect the ability to compare the ratio of numbers of letters in a game to the ratios found in the investigation.
- Sample answer: Three- and four-letter words are most common.

Interdisciplinary Investigation

(Student Edition, Pages 264–265)

"A" is for Apple

Level	Specific Criteria
3 Superior	• Shows a thorough understanding of the concept of *ratio*. • Uses appropriate strategies to solve problems. • Computations are correct. • Written explanations are exemplary. • Letter set is appropriate and sensible. • Goes beyond the requirements of some or all problems.
2 Satisfactory, with minor flaws	• Shows understanding of the concept of *ratio*. • Uses appropriate strategies to solve problems. • Computations are mostly correct. • Written explanations are effective. • Letter set is appropriate and sensible. • Satisfies the requirements of problems.
1 Nearly Satisfactory, with obvious flaws	• Shows understanding of most of the concept of *ratio*. • May not use appropriate strategies to solve problems. • Computations are mostly correct. • Written explanations are satisfactory. • Letter set is appropriate and sensible. • Satisfies the requirements of problems.
0 Unsatisfactory	• Shows little or no understanding of the concept of *ratio*. • Does not use appropriate strategies to solve problems. • Computations are incorrect. • Written explanations are not satisfactory. • Letter set is not appropriate or sensible. • Does not satisfy the requirements of the problems.

Interdisciplinary Investigation

(Student Edition, Pages 264–265)

"A" is for Apple

2.

Letter	Number of Times in Text	Ratio Out of ____ Letters	Ratio as %
A			
B			
C			
D			
E			
F			
G			
H			
I			
J			
K			
L			
M			
N			
O			
P			
Q			
R			
S			
T			
U			
V			
W			
X			
Y			
Z			

3. Most common:

Least common:

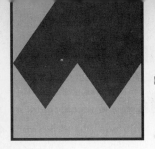

Interdisciplinary Investigation

(Student Edition, Pages 404–405)

Pi for Polygons

MATERIALS

- Recording Sheet master, p. 12
- protractor
- ruler
- compass
- construction paper
- calculator

OVERVIEW

In this investigation, students will construct and measure regular polygons and investigate the relationship between their radii and their perimeters. Make a copy of the Recording Sheet master on page 12 for each student.

PROCEDURE

1. Provide pictures of regular polygons for the purpose of example and discussion. Here are some possible discussion questions.
   - What makes a polygon regular?
   - Can you make a regular polygon out of any number of sides?
   - Have you noticed that as you increase the number of sides of a polygon, the shape looks more like a circle?
2. Emphasize that students should measure as precisely as possible to obtain accurate results. Encourage students to measure the final construction to test its accuracy.
3. You might remind students of the relationship between the radius of a circle and pi.

OUTSIDE RESOURCES

Adler, David A. *Shape Up!* New York, NY: Holiday House, 1998.
Hansen, Vagn Lundsgaard. *Geometry in Nature*. Boston, MA: Jones and Bartlett Publishers, 1992.
Stienecker, David. *Polygons*. New York, NY: Benchmark Books, 1997.

Interdisciplinary Investigation

(Student Edition, Pages 404–405)

Pi for Polygons

PROCEDURE

3. Sample answer:

Polygon	Number of Sides	Perimeter, P (in.)	Radius, r (in.)	$2r$ (in.)	$\frac{P}{2r}$
Triangle	3	3	$\frac{5}{8}$	$1\frac{1}{4}$	2.4
Square	4	4	$\frac{11}{16}$	$1\frac{3}{8}$	2.91
Pentagon	5	5	$\frac{7}{8}$	$1\frac{3}{4}$	2.86
Hexagon	6	6	1	2	3
Heptagon	7	7	$1\frac{1}{8}$	$2\frac{1}{4}$	3.11
Octagon	8	8	$1\frac{5}{16}$	$2\frac{5}{8}$	3.05
Nonagon	9	9	$1\frac{7}{16}$	$2\frac{7}{8}$	3.13
Decagon	10	10	$1\frac{5}{8}$	$3\frac{1}{4}$	3.08

4. The values in the last column of each group's table should be similar.
5. Check students' formulas for accuracy.

MAKING THE CONNECTION

Language Arts   Posters should be complete and should contain thoughtful explanations for the formulas.

Social Studies   The research should include a discussion of how, at the age of 19, Gauss was the first to use a compass and a ruler to construct a regular 17-sided polygon. A regular 17-sided polygon is called a heptadecagon.

Science   Many insects have large compound eyes that are made up of thousands of small hexagonal units. Many molecules in nature also have the shape of regular polygons.

GO FURTHER

● The ratio will get closer and closer to pi as the number of sides increases.

● As the number of sides increases, the measure of the angle increases.

Mathematics: Applications and Connections, Course 2

Interdisciplinary Investigation

(Student Edition, Pages 404–405)

Pi for Polygons

Level	Specific Criteria
3 Superior	<ul><li>Shows a thorough understanding of the concepts of *constructing regular polygons* and *working with ratios.*</li><li>Uses appropriate strategies to solve problems.</li><li>Computations are correct.</li><li>Written explanations are exemplary.</li><li>Charts, model, and any statements included are appropriate and sensible.</li><li>Goes beyond the requirements of some or all problems.</li></ul>
2 Satisfactory, with minor flaws	<ul><li>Shows understanding of the concepts of *constructing regular polygons* and *working with ratios.*</li><li>Uses appropriate strategies to solve problems.</li><li>Computations are mostly correct.</li><li>Written explanations are effective.</li><li>Charts, model, and any statements included are appropriate and sensible.</li><li>Satisfies the requirements of problems.</li></ul>
1 Nearly Satisfactory, with obvious flaws	<ul><li>Shows understanding of most of the concepts of *constructing regular polygons* and *working with ratios.*</li><li>May not use appropriate strategies to solve problems.</li><li>Computations are mostly correct.</li><li>Written explanations are satisfactory.</li><li>Charts, model, and any statements included are appropriate and sensible.</li><li>Satisfies the requirements of problems.</li></ul>
0 Unsatisfactory	<ul><li>Shows little or no understanding of the concepts of *constructing regular polygons* and *working with ratios.*</li><li>Does not use appropriate strategies to solve problems.</li><li>Computations are incorrect.</li><li>Written explanations are not satisfactory.</li><li>Charts, model, and any statements included are not appropriate or sensible.</li><li>Does not satisfy the requirements of the problems.</li></ul>

Interdisciplinary Investigation

(Student Edition, Pages 404–405)

Pi for Polygons

Use this table to record your data.

3.

Polygon	Number of Sides	Perimeter, P	Radius, r	$2r$	$\frac{P}{2r}$
	3				
	4				
	5				
	6				
	7				
	8				
	9				
	10				

12

Interdisciplinary Investigation

The Perfect Package

MATERIALS

- Recording Sheet master, p. 16
- packages from a supermarket or department store
- calculator
- cardboard or poster board
- ruler

OVERVIEW

In this investigation, students will find the volume and surface area of some common packages and design a package for their own product. Make a copy of the Recording Sheet master on page 16 for each student.

PROCEDURE

1. Emphasize that students should select packages for which they can calculate the surface area and volume. Encourage students to select different types of containers so that they will have data to compare with their partners. Provide sample data on one package for the purpose of example and discussion. Here are some possible discussion questions.

   - Which types of containers are the most popular?
   - What effect does packaging have on whether or not a product sells?
   - What types of products seem to be found in cylinders? in boxes?
   - What types of materials are used for packaging?

2. You may want to review how to calculate the areas of circles and rectangles and the volumes of prisms and cylinders. Remind students that surface area is calculated by adding together the areas of each surface of an object.

OUTSIDE RESOURCES

Hanlon, Joseph F. *Handbook of Package Engineering.* Lancaster, PA: Technomic Publishing Company, 1992.

Jankowski, Jerry. *Shelf Life.* San Francisco, CA: Chronicle Books, 1992.

Package Design & Brand Identity. Rockport, MA: Rockport Publishers, 1994.

Selke, Susan E. M. *Packaging and the Environment.* Lancaster, PA: Technomic Publishing Company, 1994.

Interdisciplinary Investigation

(Student Edition, Pages 524–525)

The Perfect Package

PROCEDURE

2. Sample answer:

Container	Length (in.)	Width (in.)	Height (in.)	Surface Area (in²)	Volume (in³)
cereal box	11	6.5	2	213	143
processed cheese box	8.5	2.5	2.75	103	58.4375

3–4. Sample answer:

Container	Length (in.)	Width (in.)	Height (in.)	Volume (in³)	Surf. Area (in²)
prism	11	6.5	2	143	213
cylinder	Radius = 3		5	141.3	150.72

I chose a radius and determined the area of the base. Then I adjusted the height until the volumes were similar.

5. Display should include the packages with their scale drawings and tables that include dimensions and calculations of volume and surface area.

MAKING THE CONNECTION

Language Arts   Students should include their reasons for choosing either the prism or the cylinder.

Science   Information should include the impact of packaging on the environment and how packaging materials have changed. Students should mention the availability and practicality of recycled and environmentally safe materials.

Art   Logos should be original, colorful, and creative. Presentations should include why the design was chosen and how students think it will best sell their product.

GO FURTHER

● Sample answer: The height is close to twice the width.
● Students' information should include a description of the containers, along with the volume and surface area calculations.

Mathematics: Applications and Connections, Course 2

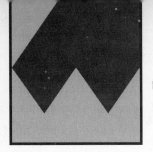

Interdisciplinary Investigation

(Student Edition, Pages 524–525)

The Perfect Package

Level	Specific Criteria
3 Superior	● Shows a thorough understanding of the concepts of *calculating surface area and volume of rectangular prisms and cylinders.*
	● Uses appropriate strategies to solve problems.
	● Computations are correct.
	● Written explanations are exemplary.
	● Charts, model, and any statements included are appropriate and sensible.
	● Goes beyond the requirements of some or all problems.
2 Satisfactory, with minor flaws	● Shows understanding of the concepts of *calculating surface area and volume of rectangular prisms and cylinders.*
	● Uses appropriate strategies to solve problems.
	● Computations are mostly correct.
	● Written explanations are effective.
	● Charts, model, and any statements included are appropriate and sensible.
	● Satisfies the requirements of problems.
1 Nearly Satisfactory, with obvious flaws	● Shows understanding of most of the *concepts of calculating surface area and volume of rectangular prisms and cylinders.*
	● May not use appropriate strategies to solve problems.
	● Computations are mostly correct.
	● Written explanations are satisfactory.
	● Charts, model, and any statements included are appropriate and sensible.
	● Satisfies the requirements of problems.
0 Unsatisfactory	● Shows little or no understanding of the concepts of *calculating surface area and volume of rectangular prisms and cylinders.*
	● Does not use appropriate strategies to solve problems.
	● Computations are incorrect.
	● Written explanations are not satisfactory.
	● Charts, model, and any statements included are not appropriate or sensible.
	● Does not satisfy the requirements of the problems.

Interdisciplinary Investigation

(Student Edition, Pages 524–525)

The Perfect Package

Use this table to record your data.

2.

Container	Length	Width	Height	Surface Area	Volume

3.

Container	Length	Width	Height	Volume
prism				
cylinder	Radius =			

4.

Container	Surface Area
prism	
cylinder	

Chapter 1 Project

Fun Ways to be Fit

MATERIALS

- Recording Sheet master, p. 20

OVERVIEW

In this project, students will use the four-step plan to design a week-long program of fitness. Make a copy of the Recording Sheet master on page 20 for each student.

MATHEMATICAL OVERVIEW

This project utilizes the following mathematical skills and concepts from Chapter 1.

- Use the four-step plan to solve problems.
- Evaluate expressions using the order of operations.
- Solve equations using mental math.

OUTSIDE RESOURCES

Franks, B. Don, and Edward T. Howley. *Fitness Facts: The Healthy Living Handbook.* Champaign, IL: Human Kinetics, 1989.

Schlosberg, Suzanne, and Liz Neporent. *Fitness for Dummies.* Foster City, CA: IDG Books Worldwide, Inc., 1996.

Sharkey, Brian J. *Fitness and Health.* 4th ed. Champaign, IL: Human Kinetics, 1997.

Chapter 1 Project

Fun Ways to be Fit

Page 3, Getting Started

- Least - sleeping, watching TV
  Most - running
  One hour of in-line skating burns 400 Calories for a 100-lb person.
- All the activities except sleeping and watching TV will burn the 287 Calories in an hour.

Page 7, Working on the Chapter Project, Exercise 11

Sample answer: Bicycling and in-line skating would burn 708 + 600 or 1,308 Calories.

Page 10, Working on the Chapter Project, Exercise 37

Sample answer: For 150 pounds, sleep for 8 hours, in-line skate for 2 hours, and swim for 1 hour: $8 \times 90 + 2 \times 600 + 1 \times 497 = 2,417$.

Page 23, Working on the Chapter Project, Exercise 40

$600h = 2,400; h = 4$

Chapter 1 Project

Fun Ways to be Fit

Level	Specific Criteria
3 Superior	● Shows a thorough understanding of the concepts of *using the four-step plan to solve problems, evaluating expressions using the order of operations,* and *solving equations mentally.* ● Uses appropriate strategies to solve problems. ● Computations are correct. ● Written explanations are exemplary. ● Goes beyond the requirements of some or all problems.
2 Satisfactory, with minor flaws	● Shows understanding of the concepts of *using the four-step plan to solve problems, evaluating expressions using the order of operations,* and *solving equations mentally.* ● Uses appropriate strategies to solve problems. ● Computations are mostly correct. ● Written explanations are effective. ● Satisfies the requirements of problems.
1 Nearly Satisfactory, with obvious flaws	● Shows understanding of most of the concepts of *using the four-step plan to solve problems, evaluating expressions using the order of operations,* and *solving equations mentally.* ● May not use appropriate strategies to solve problems. ● Computations are mostly correct. ● Written explanations are satisfactory. ● Satisfies the requirements of problems.
0 Unsatisfactory	● Shows little or no understanding of the concepts of *using the four-step plan to solve problems, evaluating expressions using the order of operations,* and *solving equations mentally.* ● Does not use appropriate strategies to solve problems. ● Computations are incorrect. ● Written explanations are not satisfactory. ● Does not satisfy the requirements of the problems.

Chapter 1 Project

Fun Ways to be Fit

Page 7, Working on the Chapter Project, Exercise 11

Activity	Calories Burned
Total	

Page 10, Working on the Chapter Project, Exercise 37

Activity	Time (h)	Calories Burned
Total		

Expression _____ = _____ Total Calories Burned

Chapter 2 Project

How Big Is Our Solar System?

MATERIALS

- Styrofoam, modeling clay, balls, marbles, or balloons
- Recording Sheet master, p. 24

OVERVIEW

In this project, students will analyze data to construct a model of our solar system using materials of their own choosing. Make a copy of the Recording Sheet master on page 24 for each student.

MATHEMATICAL OVERVIEW

This project utilizes the following mathematical skills and concepts from Chapter 2.

- Compare decimals.
- Round decimals.
- Multiply with decimals.
- Measure with metric units.

OUTSIDE RESOURCES

Branley, Franklyn. *The Sun and the Solar System.* New York: Twenty-First Century Books, 1996.

Levy, David H. *Stars and Planets.* Alexandria, VA: Time-Life Books, 1996.

Walker, Jane. *Fascinating Facts About. . . the Solar System.* Brookfield, CT: Millbrook Press, 1995.

Chapter 2 Project

How Big Is Our Solar System?

Page 43, Getting Started

- 11.19 times as big
- Neptune

Page 46, Working on the Chapter Project, Exercise 28

Page 59, Working on the Chapter Project, Exercise 32

Page 76, Working on the Chapter Project, Exercise 27

a.

Planet	Diameter	Actual Diameter (km)	Diameter (cm)
Jupiter	11.19	142,740	11.19
Saturn	9.46	120,672	9.46
Uranus	4.01	51,152	4.01
Neptune	3.88	49,493	3.88
Earth	1.00	12,756	1.00
Venus	0.95	12,118	0.95
Mars	0.53	6,761	0.53
Mercury	0.38	4,847	0.38
Pluto	0.18	2,296	0.18

b.

Planet	Distance from Sun	Actual Average Distance (million km)	Distance (cm)
Pluto	39.529	5,890	39.529
Neptune	30.061	4,479	30.061
Uranus	19.191	2,859	19.191
Saturn	9.529	1,420	9.529
Jupiter	5.203	775	5.203
Mars	1.524	227	1.524
Earth	1.000	149	1.000
Venus	0.723	108	0.723
Mercury	0.387	58	0.387

c. See students' work.

Chapter 2 Project

How Big Is Our Solar System?

Level	Specific Criteria
3 Superior	• Shows a thorough understanding of the concepts of *comparing, rounding,* and *estimating with decimals.* • Uses appropriate strategies to solve problems. • Computations are correct. • Written explanations are exemplary. • Charts, model, and any statements included are appropriate and sensible. • Goes beyond the requirements of some or all problems.
2 Satisfactory, with minor flaws	• Shows understanding of the concepts of *comparing, rounding,* and *estimating with decimals.* • Uses appropriate strategies to solve problems. • Computations are mostly correct. • Written explanations are effective. • Charts, model, and any statements included are appropriate and sensible. • Satisfies the requirements of problems.
1 Nearly Satisfactory, with obvious flaws	• Shows understanding of most of the concepts of *comparing, rounding,* and *estimating with decimals.* • May not use appropriate strategies to solve problems. • Computations are mostly correct. • Written explanations are satisfactory. • Charts, model, and any statements included are appropriate and sensible. • Satisfies the requirements of problems.
0 Unsatisfactory	• Shows little or no understanding of the concepts of *comparing, rounding,* and *estimating with decimals.* • Does not use appropriate strategies to solve problems. • Computations are incorrect. • Written explanations are not satisfactory. • Charts, model, and any statements included are not appropriate or sensible. • Does not satisfy the requirements of the problems.

23

Mathematics: Applications and Connections, Course 2

Chapter 2 Project

How Big Is Our Solar System?

Page 46, Working on the Chapter Project, Exercise 28

Page 59, Working on the Chapter Project, Exercise 32

Page 76, Working on the Chapter Project, Exercise 27

a.

Planet	Diameter	Actual Diameter (km)	Diameter (cm)

b.

Planet	Distance from Sun	Actual Average Distance (million km)	Distance (cm)

Chapter 3 Project

Lights! Camera! Action!

MATERIALS

- Recording Sheet master, p. 28

OVERVIEW

In this project, students will present statistical information on movie ticket sales and movie popularity. Students will conduct their own survey of favorite movies and create a graphic display. Make a copy of the Recording Sheet master on page 28 for each student.

MATHEMATICAL OVERVIEW

This project utilizes the following mathematical skills and concepts from Chapter 3.

- Construct frequency tables.
- Calculate median and mode for a set of data.
- Recognize misleading graphs and statistics.

OUTSIDE RESOURCES

Drummond, Lee. *American Dreamtime.* Lanham, MD: Littlefield Adams Books, 1996.
Matthews, Charles E. *Oscar A to Z.* New York, NY: Doubleday, 1995.
Stephens, Michael L. *Film Noir.* Jefferson, NC: McFarland, 1995.
The Entertainment Weekly Guide to the Greatest Movies Ever Made. New York, NY: Warner Books, 1994.

Chapter 3 Project

Lights! Camera! Action!

Page 105, Working on the Chapter Project, Exercise 19

Ticket Sales (millions)	
mean	$331.0
median	$310.9

Page 121, Working on the Chapter Project, Exercise 10

a. Sample answer:

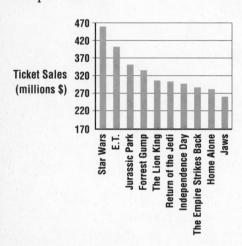

The graph is misleading because the *y*-axis starts at $170 million instead of at $0.

b. Sample answer:

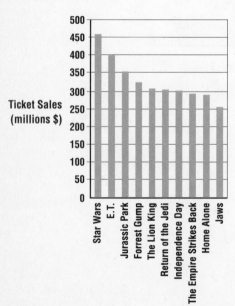

Lights! Camera! Action!

Level	Specific Criteria
3 Superior	● Shows a thorough understanding of the concepts of *creating frequency tables, calculating mean and median,* and *recognizing misleading statistics and graphs.* ● Uses appropriate strategies to solve problems. ● Computations are correct. ● Written explanations are exemplary. ● Graphs are appropriate and sensible. ● Goes beyond the requirements of some or all problems.
2 Satisfactory, with minor flaws	● Shows understanding of the concepts of *creating frequency tables, calculating mean and median,* and *recognizing misleading statistics and graphs.* ● Uses appropriate strategies to solve problems. ● Computations are mostly correct. ● Written explanations are effective. ● Graphs are appropriate and sensible. ● Satisfies the requirements of problems.
1 Nearly Satisfactory, with obvious flaws	● Shows understanding of most of the concepts of *creating frequency tables, calculating mean and median,* and *recognizing misleading statistics and graphs.* ● May not use appropriate strategies to solve problems. ● Computations are mostly correct. ● Written explanations are satisfactory. ● Graphs are appropriate and sensible. ● Satisfies the requirements of problems.
0 Unsatisfactory	● Shows little or no understanding of the concepts of *creating frequency tables, calculating mean and median,* and *recognizing misleading statistics and graphs.* ● Does not use appropriate strategies to solve problems. ● Computations are incorrect. ● Written explanations are not satisfactory. ● Graphs are not appropriate or sensible. ● Does not satisfy the requirements of the problems.

Chapter 3 Project

Lights! Camera! Action!

Page 91, Working on the Chapter Project, Exercise 22

Top 10 Movies	Tally	Frequency

Page 105, Working on the Chapter Project, Exercise 19

Ticket Sales (millions)	
mean	
median	

Page 121, Working on the Chapter Project, Exercise 10

a.

Ticket Sales
(millions $)

Star Wars • E.T. • Jurassic Park • Forrest Gump • The Lion King • Return of the Jedi • Independence Day • The Empire Strikes Back • Home Alone • Jaws

b.

Ticket Sales
(millions $)

Star Wars • E.T. • Jurassic Park • Forrest Gump • The Lion King • Return of the Jedi • Independence Day • The Empire Strikes Back • Home Alone • Jaws

Chapter 4 Project

What Color Was That Car?

MATERIALS

● Recording Sheet master, p. 32

OVERVIEW

In this project, students will conduct a survey about favorite car colors and report important statistical information using fractions, decimals, and percents. Make a copy of the Recording Sheet master on page 32 for each student.

MATHEMATICAL OVERVIEW

This project utilizes the following mathematical skills and concepts from Chapter 4.

● Express fractions in simplest form.
● Express fractions as decimals and percents.
● Find the probability of a simple event.

OUTSIDE RESOURCES

Fettis, Gordon, ed. *Automotive Paints and Coatings.* Weinheim, New York, NY: VCH, 1995.

Gage, John. *Color and Culture.* Boston, MA: Little, Brown and Company, 1993.

Maund, Barry. *Colours: Their Nature and Representation.* Cambridge: Cambridge University Press, 1995.

Quiller, Stephen. *Color Choices.* New York, NY: Watson-Guptill Publications, 1989.

Chapter 4 Project

What Color Was That Car?

Page 131, Getting Started

- General Motors Corp. produced the greatest number of cars. There were 6,350,733 cars produced in 1995.
- Students will complete the table for 20 people. See students' work.

Page 157, Working on the Chapter Project, Exercise 34

U.S. Car Production, 1995

Company	Number of Cars	Fraction	Decimal	Percent
Auto Alliance	100,000	$\frac{1}{60}$	0.02	2%
Chrysler Corp.	600,000	$\frac{1}{10}$	0.1	10%
Ford Motor Company	1,400,000	$\frac{7}{30}$	0.23	23%
General Motors Corp.	2,500,000	$\frac{5}{12}$	0.42	42%
Honda	600,000	$\frac{1}{10}$	0.1	10%
Mitsubishi	200,000	$\frac{1}{30}$	0.03	3%
Nissan	300,000	$\frac{1}{20}$	0.05	5%
Subaru Legacy	100,000	$\frac{1}{60}$	0.02	2%
Toyota	500,000	$\frac{1}{12}$	0.08	8%
Other	0	0	0.0	0%

Page 164, Working on the Chapter Project, Exercise 43

See the decimal and percent columns in the table above.

Page 168, Working on the Chapter Project, Exercise 26

See students' work. Answer should reflect students' survey results. The probability that a new student's favorite car color will be white is the number of people who selected white as their favorite car color divided by the total number of people surveyed.

Chapter 4 Project

What Color Was That Car?

Level	Specific Criteria
3 Superior	• Shows a thorough understanding of the concepts of *expressing fractions in simplest form, expressing fractions as decimals and percents,* and *finding the probability of simple events.* • Uses appropriate strategies to solve problems. • Computations are correct. • Written explanations are exemplary. • Charts are appropriate and sensible. • Goes beyond the requirements of some or all problems.
2 Satisfactory, with minor flaws	• Shows understanding of the concepts of *expressing fractions in simplest form, expressing fractions as decimals and percents,* and *finding the probability of simple events.* • Uses appropriate strategies to solve problems. • Computations are mostly correct. • Written explanations are effective. • Charts are appropriate and sensible. • Satisfies the requirements of problems.
1 Nearly Satisfactory, with obvious flaws	• Shows understanding of most of the concepts of *expressing fractions in simplest form, expressing fractions as decimals and percents,* and *finding the probability of simple events.* • May not use appropriate strategies to solve problems. • Computations are mostly correct. • Written explanations are satisfactory. • Charts are appropriate and sensible. • Satisfies the requirements of problems.
0 Unsatisfactory	• Shows little or no understanding of the concepts of *expressing fractions in simplest form, expressing fractions as decimals and percents,* and *finding the probability of simple events.* • Does not use appropriate strategies to solve problems. • Computations are incorrect. • Written explanations are not satisfactory. • Charts are not appropriate or sensible. • Does not satisfy the requirements of the problems.

Chapter 4 Project

What Color Was That Car?

Page 131, Getting Started

Name	Color				Other	Name	Color				Other

Page 157, Working on Chapter Project, Exercise 34

Page 164, Working on Chapter Project, Exercise 43

U.S. Car Production, 1995

Company	Number of Cars	Number to Nearest Hundred Thousand	Fraction	Decimal	Percent
Auto Alliance	149,562				
Chrysler Corp.	576,846				
Ford Motor Company	1,395,710				
General Motors Corp.	2,515,136				
Honda	552,995				
Mitsubishi	218,161				
Nissan	333,234				
Subaru Legacy	80,660				
Toyota	516,557				
Other	11,872				

Page 168, Working on Chapter Project, Exercise 26

The probability of a new student selecting a white car is:

Chapter 5 Project

Latitude vs. Temperature

MATERIALS

- Recording Sheet master, p. 36

OVERVIEW

In this project, students will collect and analyze data to determine the relationship between the latitude and temperatures of cities in the United States. Make a copy of the Recording Sheet master on page 36 for each student.

MATHEMATICAL OVERVIEW

This project utilizes the following mathematical skills and concepts from Chapter 5.

- Compare and order integers.
- Graph points on a coordinate plane.
- Subtract integers.

OUTSIDE RESOURCES

Lyons, Walter A. *The Handy Weather Answer Book.* Detroit, MI: Visible Ink Press, 1997.

Varawa, Joana McIntyre. *Changes in Latitude.* New York, NY: Perennial Library, 1990.

Weiss, Harvey. *Maps: Getting from Here to There.* Boston: Houghton Mifflin Company, 1991.

Chapter 5 Project

Latitude vs. Temperature

Page 183, Getting Started

- New York City and Atlanta had the highest temperatures and Fairbanks had the lowest.

- Honolulu is the closest to the equator, and Fairbanks is the farthest from the equator.

Page 190, Working on the Chapter Project, Exercise 25

a.

City	Latitude	Low Temp. (°F)
Honolulu, HI	21°	56
San Diego, CA	33°	43
Atlanta, GA	34°	13
Nashville, TN	36°	9
Denver, CO	40°	−7
New York, NY	41°	6
Minneapolis, MN	45°	−11
Bismarck, ND	47°	−28
Seattle, WA	48°	22
Fairbanks, AK	65°	−48

b. Generally, as the latitude increases, the low temperature decreases.

Page 194, Working on the Chapter Project, Exercise 33

a. Honolulu, (21, 56); San Diego, (33, 43); Atlanta, (34, 13); Nashville, (36, 9); Denver, (40, −7); New York, (41, 6); Minneapolis, (45, −11); Bismarck, (47, −28); Seattle, (48, 22); Fairbanks, (65, −48)

b.

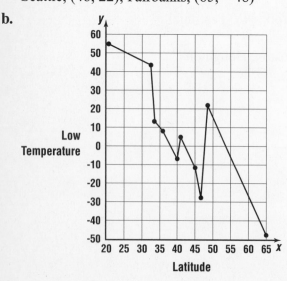

Page 205, Working on the Chapter Project, Exercise 45

a. Honolulu, (21, 38); San Diego, (33, 47); Atlanta, (34, 89); Nashville, (36, 90); Denver, (40, 106); New York, (41, 96); Minneapolis, (45, 112); Bismarck, (47, 126); Seattle, (48, 74); Fairbanks, (65, 136)

b.

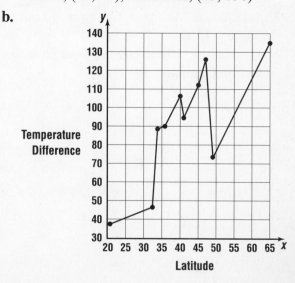

Mathematics: Applications and Connections, Course 2

Chapter 5 Project

Latitude vs. Temperature

Level	Specific Criteria
3 Superior	• Shows a thorough understanding of the concepts of *comparing and ordering integers, subtracting integers,* and *graphing points on a coordinate plane.* • Uses appropriate strategies to solve problems. • Computations are correct. • Written explanations are exemplary. • Tables and graphs are appropriate and sensible. • Goes beyond the requirements of some or all problems.
2 Satisfactory, with minor flaws	• Shows understanding of the concepts of *comparing and ordering integers, subtracting integers,* and *graphing points on a coordinate plane.* • Uses appropriate strategies to solve problems. • Computations are mostly correct. • Written explanations are effective. • Tables and graphs are appropriate and sensible. • Satisfies the requirements of problems.
1 Nearly Satisfactory, with obvious flaws	• Shows understanding of most of the concepts of *comparing and ordering integers, subtracting integers,* and *graphing points on a coordinate plane.* • May not use appropriate strategies to solve problems. • Computations are mostly correct. • Written explanations are satisfactory. • Tables and graphs are appropriate and sensible. • Satisfies the requirements of problems.
0 Unsatisfactory	• Shows little or no understanding of the concepts of *comparing and ordering integers, subtracting integers,* and *graphing points on a coordinate plane.* • Does not use appropriate strategies to solve problems. • Computations are incorrect. • Written explanations are not satisfactory. • Tables and graphs are not appropriate or sensible. • Does not satisfy the requirements of the problems.

Chapter 5 Project

Latitude vs. Temperature

Page 190, Working on the Chapter Project, Exercise 25

City	Latitude	Low Temp. (°F)

Page 194, Working on the Chapter Project, Exercise 33

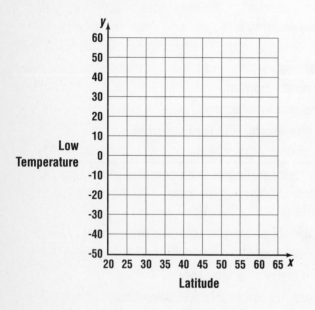

Page 205, Working on the Chapter Project, Exercise 45

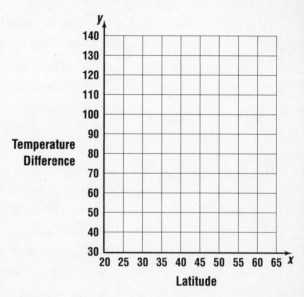

Chapter 6 Project

America's Scream Machines

MATERIALS

● Recording Sheet master, p. 40

OVERVIEW

In this project, students will use equations to calculate average speeds of roller coasters. Students will choose one of the roller coasters and graph the distance it travels and the number of riders it can carry. Make a copy of the Recording Sheet master on page 40 for each student.

MATHEMATICAL OVERVIEW

This project utilizes the following mathematical skills and concepts from Chapter 6.

● Solve multiplication equations.

● Represent functions as ordered pairs.

● Graph functions.

OUTSIDE RESOURCES

Alter, Judy. *Amusement Parks*. New York, NY: F. Watts, 1997.

Chandler, Gil. *Roller Coasters*. Minneapolis, MN: Capstone Press, 1995.

Throgmorton, Todd H. *Roller Coaster of America*. Osceola, WI: Motorbooks International, 1994.

Urbanowicz, Steven J. *The Roller Coaster Lover's Companion*. Secaucus, NJ: Carol Publishing Group, 1997.

Chapter 6 Project

America's Scream Machines

Page 225, Getting Started

- The Mean Streak travels the greatest distance and the Wildcat takes the least amount of time.

- The Gemini can accommodate the greatest number of riders per hour.

Page 236, Working on the Chapter Project, Exercise 32

a. **Roller Coasters at Cedar Point**

Name	Avg. Speed (ft/s)
Blue Streak	24
Cedar Creek	16
Corkscrew	17
Gemini	28
Iron Dragon	23
Magnum	43
Mantis	24
Mean Streak	33
Raptor	28
Wildcat	22

b. Sample answer:

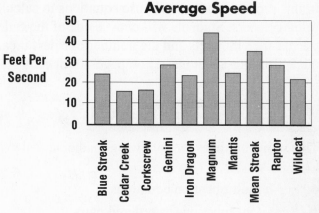

Page 252, Working on the Chapter Project, Exercise 8

Answers will vary depending on the coaster selected. Sample answer for Magnum is given.

a. Ordered pairs: (1, 43); (2, 86); (3, 129); (4, 172); (5, 215); (6, 258); (7, 301); (8, 344); (9, 387); (10, 430)

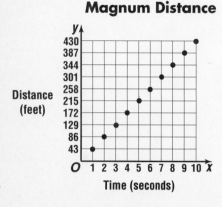

b. Yes, the average distance increases with time.

Page 257, Working on the Chapter Project, Exercise 30

Answers will vary depending on the coaster selected. Sample answer for Magnum is given.

a. Ordered pairs: (1, 2,000); (2, 4,000); (3, 6,000); (4, 8,000); (5, 10,000); (6, 12,000); (7, 14,000); (8, 16,000); (9, 18,000); (10, 20,000); (11, 22,000); (12, 24,000)

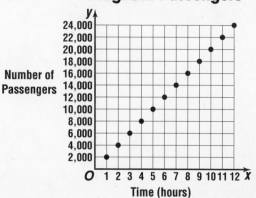

b. $y = 2,000x$

America's Scream Machines

Level	Specific Criteria
3 Superior	• Shows a thorough understanding of the concepts of *solving multiplication equations, representing functions as ordered pairs,* and *graphing functions.* • Uses appropriate strategies to solve problems. • Computations are correct. • Written explanations are exemplary. • Tables and graphs are appropriate and sensible. • Goes beyond the requirements of some or all problems.
2 Satisfactory, with minor flaws	• Shows understanding of the concepts of *solving multiplication equations, representing functions as ordered pairs,* and *graphing functions.* • Uses appropriate strategies to solve problems. • Computations are mostly correct. • Written explanations are effective. • Tables and graphs are appropriate and sensible. • Satisfies the requirements of problems.
1 Nearly Satisfactory, with obvious flaws	• Shows understanding of most of the concepts of *solving multiplication equations, representing functions as ordered pairs,* and *graphing functions.* • May not use appropriate strategies to solve problems. • Computations are mostly correct. • Written explanations are satisfactory. • Tables and graphs are appropriate and sensible. • Satisfies the requirements of problems.
0 Unsatisfactory	• Shows little or no understanding of the concepts of *solving multiplication equations, representing functions as ordered pairs,* and *graphing functions.* • Does not use appropriate strategies to solve problems. • Computations are incorrect. • Written explanations are not satisfactory. • Tables and graphs are not appropriate or sensible. • Does not satisfy the requirements of the problems.

Chapter 6 Project

America's Scream Machines

Page 225, Getting Started

The _____ travels the greatest distance.

The _____ takes the least amount of time.

The _____ can accommodate the greatest number
of riders per hour.

Page 236, Working on the Chapter Project, Exercise 32

a. Roller Coasters at Cedar Point   **b.**

Name	Avg. Speed (ft/s)
Blue Streak	
Cedar Creek	
Corkscrew	
Gemini	
Iron Dragon	
Magnum	
Mantis	
Mean Streak	
Raptor	
Wildcat	

Average Speed

Feet Per Second

Blue Streak | Cedar Creek | Corkscrew | Gemini | Iron Dragon | Magnum | Mantis | Mean Streak | Raptor | Wildcat

Page 252, Working on the Chapter Project, Exercise 8

a. Ordered pairs:

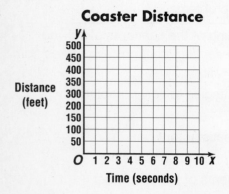

Coaster Distance

Distance (feet)

Time (seconds)

b.

Page 257, Working on the Chapter Project, Exercise 30

a. Ordered pairs:

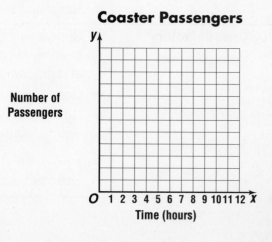

Coaster Passengers

Number of Passengers

Time (hours)

b.

Mathematics: Applications and Connections, Course 2

Chapter 7 Project

Ups and Downs

MATERIALS

● Recording Sheet master, p. 44

OVERVIEW

In this project, students will select and follow four companies in the stock market. They will calculate gains and losses over a period of one month and report on their companies' stock history. Make a copy of the Recording Sheet master on page 44 for each student.

MATHEMATICAL OVERVIEW

This project utilizes the following mathematical skills and concepts from Chapter 7.

● Estimate products.

● Multiply fractions and mixed numbers.

● Divide fractions and mixed numbers.

OUTSIDE RESOURCES

Cook, Wade. *Stock Market Miracles*. Kent, WA: Lighthouse Publishing, 1997.

Fosback, Norman G. *Stock Market Logic*. Chicago: Dearborn Financial Publishing, 1992.

Sheimo, Michael D. *Stock Market Rules*. Chicago, IL: Probus, 1991.

Teweles, Richard Jack. *The Stock Market*. New York: Wiley, 1992.

Chapter 7 Project

Ups and Downs

Page 267, Getting Started

Students will complete a similar table and track their companies for one month.

Company	M	T	W	Th	F	M
Gap	50 3/8	51 7/8	50 7/8	52	52 3/8	...
Mattel	34 3/16	34 1/16	33 7/8	34 1/2	34 7/8	...
McDonald's	46 3/4	46 3/8	46 1/8	46 3/4	46 11/16	...
Sony	98 1/4	98 3/8	98	98 1/8	98 1/2	...

Page 271, Working on the Chapter Project, Exercise 51

Sample answer: The estimated cost of buying 32 shares of Mattel stock on August 18, 1997, was $1,082.00.

Page 287, Working on the Chapter Project, Exercise 36

a. Sample answer is based on the table above tracking four companies for one week. Students' answers will reflect one month of tracking.

Company	Cost for 100 Shares (August 18, 1997)	Cost for 100 Shares (On Another Day)
Gap	$5,037.50	$5,237.50
Mattel	$3,418.75	$3,487.50
McDonald's	$4,675.00	$4,668.75
Sony	$9,825.00	$9,850.00

b. I would have received $287.50 by selling my shares.

Page 307, Working on the Chapter Project, Exercise 35

Sample answer is based on the closing price of the stock according to the above table reflecting one week of trading.

a. I could have purchased 29 shares of Mattel stock on August 18, 1997, for $980.56.

b. Sample answer: $1,011.38.

Chapter 7 Project

Ups and Downs

Level	Specific Criteria
3 Superior	● Shows a thorough understanding of the concepts of *estimating products* and *multiplying and dividing fractions and mixed numbers.* ● Uses appropriate strategies to solve problems. ● Computations are correct. ● Written explanations are exemplary. ● Tables included are appropriate and sensible. ● Goes beyond the requirements of some or all problems.
2 Satisfactory, with minor flaws	● Shows understanding of the concepts of *estimating products* and *multiplying and dividing fractions and mixed numbers.* ● Uses appropriate strategies to solve problems. ● Computations are mostly correct. ● Written explanations are effective. ● Tables included are appropriate and sensible. ● Satisfies the requirements of problems.
1 Nearly Satisfactory, with obvious flaws	● Shows understanding of most of the concepts of *estimating products* and *multiplying and dividing fractions and mixed numbers.* ● May not use appropriate strategies to solve problems. ● Computations are mostly correct. ● Written explanations are satisfactory. ● Tables included are appropriate and sensible. ● Satisfies the requirements of problems.
0 Unsatisfactory	● Shows little or no understanding of the concepts of *estimating products* and *multiplying and dividing fractions and mixed numbers.* ● Does not use appropriate strategies to solve problems. ● Computations are incorrect. ● Written explanations are not satisfactory. ● Tables included are not appropriate or sensible. ● Does not satisfy the requirements of the problems.

Chapter 7 Project

Ups and Downs

Page 267, Getting Started

Make your own table on a separate sheet of paper.

Page 271, Working on the Chapter Project, Exercise 51

The estimated cost of buying 32 shares of _____ stock on August 18, 1997, was _____.

Page 287, Working on the Chapter Project, Exercise 36

a.

Company	Cost for 100 Shares (First Day)	Cost for 100 Shares (Yesterday)

b.

Page 307, Working on the Chapter Project, Exercise 35

a.

b.

Chapter 8 Project

Waste Not, Want Not

MATERIALS

- Recording Sheet master, p. 48
- miscellaneous supplies for poster construction
- information, articles, and business portions of phone directories to collect data about recycling

OVERVIEW

In this project, students will construct a poster about trash recycling. It will include information about ways students can reduce the amount of trash their family produces. The information will be recorded in the form of fractions and percents to demonstrate the impact of recycling on trash reduction. Make a copy of the Recording Sheet master on page 48 for each student.

MATHEMATICAL OVERVIEW

This project utilizes the following mathematical skills and concepts from Chapter 8.

- Solve problems using the percent proportion.
- Find the percent of decrease.

OUTSIDE RESOURCES

Branson, Gary D. *The Complete Guide to Recycling at Home.* White Hall, VA: Betterway Publications, 1991.

Carless, Jennifer. *Taking Out the Trash.* Washington, DC: Island Press, 1992.

McVicker, Dee. *Easy Recycling Handbook.* Gilbert, AZ: Grassroots Books, 1994.

Chapter 8 Project

Waste Not, Want Not

Page 315, Getting Started

Sample answers:

Trash Items	Day 1	Day 2	Day 3	Day 4	Day 5	Day 6	Day 7
Paper	$\frac{7}{23}$	$\frac{1}{3}$	$\frac{5}{14}$	$\frac{9}{26}$	$\frac{2}{9}$	$\frac{5}{8}$	$\frac{7}{12}$
Napkins	$\frac{3}{23}$	$\frac{1}{6}$	$\frac{3}{14}$	$\frac{3}{26}$	$\frac{1}{6}$	$\frac{3}{8}$	$\frac{1}{4}$
Aluminum cans	$\frac{2}{23}$	$\frac{1}{18}$	$\frac{3}{14}$	$\frac{1}{13}$	$\frac{1}{6}$	0	$\frac{1}{12}$
Food wrappers	$\frac{4}{23}$	$\frac{5}{18}$	$\frac{1}{7}$	$\frac{5}{26}$	$\frac{2}{9}$	0	$\frac{1}{12}$
Paper	$\frac{6}{23}$	$\frac{1}{9}$	0	$\frac{3}{13}$	$\frac{1}{6}$	0	0
Sandwich bags	$\frac{1}{23}$	$\frac{1}{18}$	$\frac{1}{14}$	$\frac{1}{13}$	$\frac{1}{18}$	0	0

Page 320, Working on the Chapter Project, Exercise 42

Sample answers:

Trash Item	Ratio
Paper	$\frac{43}{119}$
Napkins	$\frac{3}{17}$
Aluminum cans	$\frac{12}{119}$
Food wrappers	$\frac{3}{17}$
Paper	$\frac{1}{7}$
Sandwich bags	$\frac{5}{119}$

Page 345, Working on the Chapter Project, Exercise 50

Paragraph should include a list of the recycling centers in the area along with the products that they recycle. Estimated amounts should be included, and each should be presented in a similar unit of measure and time. For example, amounts may be listed in pounds per month.

Trash Item	Pounds per Month
Paper products	13,000
Glass products	10,500
Aluminum	8,000

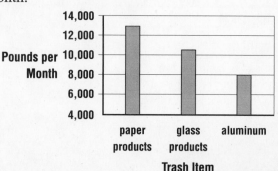

Mathematics: Applications and Connections, Course 2

Chapter 8 Project

Waste Not, Want Not

Level	Specific Criteria
3 Superior	• Shows a thorough understanding of the concepts of *solving problems using the percent proportion* and *finding the percent of decrease.* • Uses appropriate strategies to solve problems. • Computations are correct. • Written explanations are exemplary. • Charts are appropriate and sensible. • Goes beyond the requirements of some or all problems.
2 Satisfactory, with minor flaws	• Shows understanding of the concepts of *solving problems using the percent proportion* and *finding the percent of decrease.* • Uses appropriate strategies to solve problems. • Computations are mostly correct. • Written explanations are effective. • Charts are appropriate and sensible. • Satisfies the requirements of problems.
1 Nearly Satisfactory, with obvious flaws	• Shows understanding of most of the concepts of *solving problems using the percent proportion* and *finding the percent of decrease.* • May not use appropriate strategies to solve problems. • Computations are mostly correct. • Written explanations are satisfactory. • Charts are appropriate and sensible. • Satisfies the requirements of problems.
0 Unsatisfactory	• Shows little or no understanding of the concepts of *solving problems using the percent proportion* and *finding the percent of decrease.* • Does not use appropriate strategies to solve problems. • Computations are incorrect. • Written explanations are not satisfactory. • Charts are not appropriate or sensible. • Does not satisfy the requirements of the problems.

Chapter 8 Project

Waste Not, Want Not

Page 315, Getting Started

Trash Items	Day 1	Day 2	Day 3	Day 4	Day 5	Day 6	Day 7

Page 320, Working on the Chapter Project, Exercise 42

Trash Item	Ratio

Page 345, Working on the Chapter Project, Exercise 50

Pounds per Month

Trash Item

Chapter 9 Project

Geometric Art

MATERIALS

- Recording Sheet master, p. 52

OVERVIEW

In this project, students will display a creation formed from their own tessellation designs. Make a copy of the Recording Sheet master on page 52 for each student.

MATHEMATICAL OVERVIEW

This project utilizes the following mathematical skills and concepts from Chapter 9.

- Determine figures that can be used to form tessellations.
- Create tessellations using translations.
- Create tessellations using reflections.

OUTSIDE RESOURCES

Bertol, Daniela. *Visualizing with CAD.* Santa Clara, CA: Telos, 1994.

Locher, J. L., ed. *M. C. Escher: His Life and Complete Graphic Work.*
   New York: Abradale Press/Harry N. Abrams, Inc., 1992.

Tessellation Winners. Palo Alto, CA: Dale Seymour Publications, 1991.

Chapter 9 Project

Geometric Art

Page 359, Getting Started

● Sample answer: The tile pattern on the kitchen floor is a tessellation of hexagons. The pattern on the drapes covering the living room window forms a tessellation containing triangles and hexagons.

Page 391, Working on the Chapter Project, Exercise 14

Sample answer:

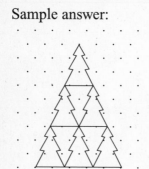

Page 394, Working on the Chapter Project, Exercise 12

Sample answer:

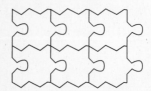

Page 397, Working on the Chapter Project, Exercise 11

Sample answer:

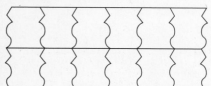

Chapter 9 Project

Geometric Art

Level	Specific Criteria
3 Superior	<ul><li>Shows a thorough understanding of the concepts of *creating tessellations, translations, and reflections.*</li><li>Uses appropriate strategies to solve problems.</li><li>Computations are correct.</li><li>Written explanations are exemplary.</li><li>Charts, model, and any statements included are appropriate and sensible.</li><li>Goes beyond the requirements of some or all problems.</li></ul>
2 Satisfactory, with minor flaws	<ul><li>Shows understanding of the concepts of *creating tessellations, translations, and reflections.*</li><li>Uses appropriate strategies to solve problems.</li><li>Computations are mostly correct.</li><li>Written explanations are effective.</li><li>Charts, model, and any statements included are appropriate and sensible.</li><li>Satisfies the requirements of problems.</li></ul>
1 Nearly Satisfactory, with obvious flaws	<ul><li>Shows understanding of most of the concepts of *creating tessellations, translations, and reflections.*</li><li>May not use appropriate strategies to solve problems.</li><li>Computations are mostly correct.</li><li>Written explanations are satisfactory.</li><li>Charts, model, and any statements included are appropriate and sensible.</li><li>Satisfies the requirements of problems.</li></ul>
0 Unsatisfactory	<ul><li>Shows little or no understanding of the concepts of *creating tessellations, translations, and reflections.*</li><li>Does not use appropriate strategies to solve problems.</li><li>Computations are incorrect.</li><li>Written explanations are not satisfactory.</li><li>Charts, model, and any statements included are not appropriate or sensible.</li><li>Does not satisfy the requirements of the problems.</li></ul>

Chapter 9 Project

Geometric Art

Page 391, Working on the Chapter Project, Exercise 14

Page 394, Working on the Chapter Project, Exercise 12

Page 397, Working on the Chapter Project, Exercise 11

Chapter 10 Project

It's a Small World

MATERIALS

- Recording Sheet master, p. 56
- poster boards ☐, colored pencils , grid paper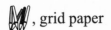

OVERVIEW

In this project, students will make a map and use estimation and calculation techniques to determine the areas of both land and water masses. Students will use their map as an area model to find probability. Make a copy of the Recording Sheet master on page 56 for each student.

MATHEMATICAL OVERVIEW

This project utilizes the following mathematical skills and concepts from Chapter 10.

- Estimate the area of irregular figures.
- Find the area of triangles and trapezoids.
- Find probability using area models.

OUTSIDE RESOURCES

Monmonier, Mark S. *Drawing the Line: Tales of Map and Cartocontroversy.* New York, NY: H. Holt, 1995.

National Geographic Atlas of the World, revised 6th ed. Washington, DC: National Geographic Society, 1996.

Pratt, Paula. *Maps: Plotting Places on the Globe.* San Diego, CA: Lucent Books, 1995.

Smoothey, Marion. *Maps and Scale Drawings.* New York, NY: Marshall-Cavendish, 1995.

Chapter 10 Project

It's a Small World

Page 407, Getting Started

See students' work. Students should have a sketch of the world with the continents and oceans labeled.

Page 426, Working on the Chapter Project, Exercise 16

Sample answer:

Landmass	Estimate of Area (sq. mi)	Actual Area (sq. mi)
North America	9,331,000	9,360,000
South America	6,620,000	6,883,000
Europe/Asia	26,884,000	21,196,000
Africa	11,034,000	11,707,000
Australia	3,121,000	3,284,000
Antarctica	5,773,000	6,000,000
Body of Water	**Estimated**	**Actual**
Pacific Ocean	69,169,000	64,000,000
Atlantic Ocean	35,357,000	31,815,000
Indian Ocean	28,941,000	25,300,000
Arctic Ocean	5,164,000	5,440,200

Page 431, Working on the Chapter Project, Exercise 24

Sample answer:

Triangles and Trapezoids		
Name	**Area**	
	Estimated	Actual
Australia	3,121,000	3,284,000
Africa	11,034,000	11,707,000
South America	6,620,000	6,883,000

Page 441, Working on the Chapter Project, Exercise 18

The probability that the meteor will land in water is about $\frac{7}{10}$.

It's a Small World

Level	Specific Criteria
3 Superior	• Shows a thorough understanding of the concepts of *estimating the area of irregular figures, finding area of triangles and trapezoids*, and *finding probability using area models.* • Uses appropriate strategies to solve problems. • Computations are correct. • Written explanations are exemplary. • Charts are appropriate and sensible. • Goes beyond the requirements of some or all problems.
2 Satisfactory, with minor flaws	• Shows understanding of the concepts of *estimating the area of irregular figures, finding area of triangles and trapezoids*, and *finding probability using area models.* • Uses appropriate strategies to solve problems. • Computations are mostly correct. • Written explanations are effective. • Charts are appropriate and sensible. • Satisfies the requirements of problems.
1 Nearly Satisfactory, with obvious flaws	• Shows understanding of most of the concepts of *estimating the area of irregular figures, finding area of triangles and trapezoids*, and *finding probability using area models.* • May not use appropriate strategies to solve problems. • Computations are mostly correct. • Written explanations are satisfactory. • Charts are appropriate and sensible. • Satisfies the requirements of problems.
0 Unsatisfactory	• Shows little or no understanding of the concepts of *estimating the area of irregular figures, finding area of triangles and trapezoids*, and *finding probability using area models.* • Does not use appropriate strategies to solve problems. • Computations are incorrect. • Written explanations are not satisfactory. • Charts are not appropriate or sensible. • Does not satisfy the requirements of the problems.

Chapter 10 Project

It's a Small World

Page 426, Working on the Chapter Project, Exercise 16

Landmass	Estimate of Area (sq. mi)	Actual Area (sq. mi)
North America		
South America		
Europe/Asia		
Africa		
Australia		
Antarctica		
Body of Water	**Estimated**	**Actual**
Pacific Ocean		
Atlantic Ocean		
Indian Ocean		
Arctic Ocean		

Page 431, Working on the Chapter Project, Exercise 24

Triangles and Trapezoids		
Name	**Area**	
	Estimated	Actual
Australia		
Africa		
South America		

Page 441, Working on the Chapter Project, Exercise 18

The probability that the meteor will land in water is about:

Chapter 11 Project

Don't Turn That Dial!

MATERIALS

● Recording Sheet master, p. 60

OVERVIEW

In this project, students will collect data about radio programming.
Students will interpret their data by using circle graphs and percents.
Make a copy of the Recording Sheet master on page 60 for each student.

MATHEMATICAL OVERVIEW

This project utilizes the following mathematical skills and concepts from
Chapter 11.

● Solve problems using the percent equation.

● Construct circle graphs.

● Predict actions of a larger group by using a sample.

OUTSIDE RESOURCES

Adams, Michael H. *Introduction to Radio.* Madison, WI:
  Brown & Benchmark, 1995.

Halper, Donna L. *Full-Service Radio.* Boston: Focal Press, 1991.

MacFarland, David T. *Contemporary Radio Programming Strategies.*
  Hillsdale, NJ: L. Erlbaum Associates, 1990.

Vane, Edwin T. *Programming for TV, Radio, and Cable.* Boston, MA: Focal
  Press, 1994.

Don't Turn That Dial!

Page 449, Getting Started

Sample answer:

Station: KRZY		
Format: Country		
Time: Tuesday, October 6, 10:00 A.M.		
Time	**Type of Programming**	**Number of Minutes**
10:00	News	5
10:05	Commercials	2
10:07	Weather	0.5
10:07	Music	22
10:29	Commercials	3
10:32	Station ID	0.5
10:33	Music	27

Page 458, Working on the Chapter Project, Exercise 25

Sample answer:

Type of Programming	Percent of Total Hour
News	8.33%
Commercials	8.33%
Weather	0.83%
Music	81.67%
Station ID	0.83%

Page 463, Working on the Chapter Project, Exercise 9

a. Sample answer:

Type of Programming

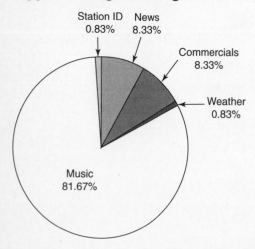

b. Summaries should include comparisons of each type of programming and should list the types of programming that were unique to some graphs.

Page 467, Working on the Chapter Project, Exercise 10

Students' programming schedules should incorporate the percents found in their sample data. Each type of programming should be included in each hour of the schedule.

Chapter 11 Project

Don't Turn That Dial!

Level	Specific Criteria
3 Superior	• Shows a thorough understanding of the concepts of *solving problems involving percent, creating circle graphs,* and *making predictions using sample data.* • Uses appropriate strategies to solve problems. • Computations are correct. • Written explanations are exemplary. • Charts are appropriate and sensible. • Goes beyond the requirements of some or all problems.
2 Satisfactory, with minor flaws	• Shows understanding of the concepts of *solving problems involving percent, creating circle graphs,* and *making predictions using sample data.* • Uses appropriate strategies to solve problems. • Computations are mostly correct. • Written explanations are effective. • Charts are appropriate and sensible. • Satisfies the requirements of problems.
1 Nearly Satisfactory, with obvious flaws	• Shows understanding of most of the concepts of *solving problems involving percent, creating circle graphs,* and *making predictions using sample data.* • May not use appropriate strategies to solve problems. • Computations are mostly correct. • Written explanations are satisfactory. • Charts are appropriate and sensible. • Satisfies the requirements of problems.
0 Unsatisfactory	• Shows little or no understanding of the concepts of *solving problems involving percent, creating circle graphs,* and *making predictions using sample data.* • Does not use appropriate strategies to solve problems. • Computations are incorrect. • Written explanations are not satisfactory. • Charts are not appropriate or sensible. • Does not satisfy the requirements of the problems.

11 Chapter 11 Project

Don't Turn That Dial!

Page 449, Getting Started

Station:		
Format:		
Time:		
Time	Type of Programming	Number of Minutes

Page 458, Working on the Chapter Project, Exercise 25

Type of Programming	Percent of Total Hour

Page 463, Working on the Chapter Project, Exercise 9

Type of Programming

Page 467, Working on the Chapter Project, Exercise 10

On a separate sheet of paper, make an 8-hour programming schedule for the radio station you chose. To help organize your schedule, make a table with the following headings: Time, Type of Programming, and Number of Minutes.

Chapter 12 Project

Turn Over A New Leaf

MATERIALS

● Recording Sheet master, p. 64

OVERVIEW

In this project, students will investigate the relationship between the volume and surface area of a leaf and discuss why that relationship exists. Make a copy of the Recording Sheet master on page 64 for each student.

MATHEMATICAL OVERVIEW

This project utilizes the following mathematical skills and concepts from Chapter 12.

● Estimate the area of irregular shapes.

● Calculate the volume of prisms.

● Calculate the surface area of prisms.

OUTSIDE RESOURCES

Burns, Diane L. *Trees, Leaves and Bark.* Milwaukee, WI: Gareth Stevens Publishing, 1998.

Burton, Jane. *The Nature and Science of Leaves.* Milwaukee, WI: Gareth Stevens Publishing, 1992.

Charman, Andy. *I Wonder Why Trees Have Leaves, and Other Questions About Plants.* New York, NY: Kingfisher, 1997.

Vitale, Alice Thoms. *Leaves.* New York, NY: Stewart, Tabori & Chang, 1997.

Chapter 12 Project

Turn Over A New Leaf

Page 489, Getting Started

● Sample answer:

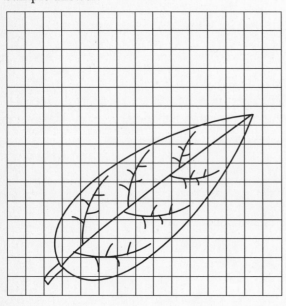

● Sample answer:
  Leaves contain chloroplasts, which aid in photosynthesis. Leaves have waxy cuticles, which help prevent water loss. They also have stomata, small pores that open and close to regulate gas exchange.

Page 501, Working on the Chapter Project, Exercise 20

Sample answer:

a. $A = 12 \text{ cm}^2$

b. $V = 1.2 \text{ cm}^3$

Page 513, Working on the Chapter Project, Exercise 17

Sample answer:

a. surface area $= 24 \text{ cm}^2$

b. The ratio of the surface area to the volume is 20:1.

Turn Over A New Leaf

Level	Specific Criteria
3 Superior	• Shows a thorough understanding of the concepts of *calculating volume and surface area of prisms.* • Uses appropriate strategies to solve problems. • Computations are correct. • Written explanations are exemplary. • Goes beyond the requirements of some or all problems.
2 Satisfactory, with minor flaws	• Shows understanding of the concepts of *calculating volume and surface area of prisms.* • Uses appropriate strategies to solve problems. • Computations are mostly correct. • Written explanations are effective. • Satisfies the requirements of problems.
1 Nearly Satisfactory, with obvious flaws	• Shows understanding of most of the concepts of *calculating volume and surface area of prisms.* • May not use appropriate strategies to solve problems. • Computations are mostly correct. • Written explanations are satisfactory. • Satisfies the requirements of problems.
0 Unsatisfactory	• Shows little or no understanding of the concepts of *calculating volume and surface area of prisms.* • Does not use appropriate strategies to solve problems. • Computations are incorrect. • Written explanations are not satisfactory. • Does not satisfy the requirements of the problems.

Name _____ Date _____

Chapter 12 Project

Turn Over A New Leaf

Page 489, Getting Started

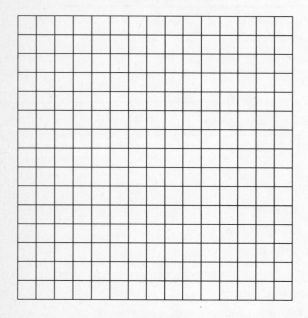

Page 501, Working on the Chapter Project, Exercise 20

a. The estimated area is:

b. The volume is:

Page 513, Working on the Chapter Project, Exercise 17

a. The surface area is:

b. The ratio of the surface area to the volume is:

Chapter 13 Project

Advance to GO and Collect $200

MATERIALS

- Recording Sheet master, p. 68

OVERVIEW

In this project, students will analyze the use of probability in a specific board game and design their own board game that combines both skill and chance. Make a copy of the Recording Sheet master on page 68 for each student.

MATHEMATICAL OVERVIEW

This project utilizes the following mathematical skills and concepts from Chapter 13.

- Find experimental and theoretical probabilities.
- Find the probability of dependent and independent events.

OUTSIDE RESOURCES

Loader, Jeff. *Making Board, Peg, & Dice Games.* Lewes, East Sussex: Guild of Master Craftsman Publications, 1993.

Polizzi, Rick. *Spin Again.* San Francisco: Chronicle Books, 1991.

Provenzo, Asterie Baker. *Favorite Board Games You Can Make and Play.* New York: Dover Publications, 1990.

Sackson, Sid. *The Book of Classic Board Games.* Palo Alto, CA: Klutz Press, 1991.

Chapter 13 Project

Advance to GO and Collect $200

Page 527, Getting Started

Students' plans should include a diagram to help explain the game design. They should state the object of the game, the number of possible players, and a brief description of the rules. They should describe the skills involved along with the way in which probability is used.

Page 533, Working on the Chapter Project, Exercise 22

Sample answer:

In the board game Candy Land®, there is a deck of 60 cards. The cards are one of six different colors and each color comes in both single and double. There are also six special cards.

On the board, there is a path of 134 colored squares. There are 123 squares that contain one of the six colors found on the cards. In addition, there are six special squares that correspond to the special cards, three penalty squares, and two advancement squares.

Probability is used in the card-drawing process and in the different types of squares on which a player may land.

Page 545, Working on the Chapter Project, Exercise 18

Sample answer: Each move is determined by both a spin of a spinner and a roll of a number cube. These events are independent.

Chapter 13 Project

Advance to GO and Collect $200

Level	Specific Criteria
3 Superior	● Shows a thorough understanding of the concepts of *identifying experimental and theoretical probabilities* and *differentiating between dependent and independent events.* ● Uses appropriate strategies to solve problems. ● Computations are correct. ● Written explanations are exemplary. ● Goes beyond the requirements of some or all problems.
2 Satisfactory, with minor flaws	● Shows understanding of the concepts of *identifying experimental and theoretical probabilities* and *differentiating between dependent and independent events.* ● Uses appropriate strategies to solve problems. ● Computations are mostly correct. ● Written explanations are effective. ● Satisfies the requirements of problems.
1 Nearly Satisfactory, with obvious flaws	● Shows understanding of most of the concepts of *identifying experimental and theoretical probabilities* and *differentiating between dependent and independent events.* ● May not use appropriate strategies to solve problems. ● Computations are mostly correct. ● Written explanations are satisfactory. ● Satisfies the requirements of problems.
0 Unsatisfactory	● Shows little or no understanding of the concepts of *identifying experimental and theoretical probabilities* and *differentiating between dependent and independent events.* ● Does not use appropriate strategies to solve problems. ● Computations are incorrect. ● Written explanations are not satisfactory. ● Does not satisfy the requirements of the problems.

Chapter 13 Project

Advance to GO and Collect $200

Page 527, Getting Started

Game diagram:

Object of the game:

Number of players:

Rules for play:

Levels of skill:

Use of probability: